Inner Life of Turtles

The Meter is Irregular

Volume 3

Roddy

1st WORLD
PUBLISHING

Inner Life of Turtles

The Meter is Irregular, Volume 3

Roddy

Published by 1st World Publishing
P.O. Box 2211, Fairfield, Iowa 52556
tel: 641-209-5000 • fax: 866-440-5234
web: www.1stworldpublishing.com

First Edition

LCCN: 2014937134

ISBN: 978-1421-8372-7-7

Acknowledgments

The friendly turtles
that taught me to discern,
surrender, love,
and then write about it.

Dedication

My sister
whom I seldom see,
think of often,
and treasure always

Preface

Again,
my imperfections are deliberate.
Apt to rush,
I comfort myself with the confidence
that I'll fix my weak prose
when my bones
no longer spring up stairways.

And
eager for love's touch,
I'll walk by your side
in warm, shady parks,
holding hands—
the true measure of poetry.

CONTENTS

Love Again

Fairfield February—
sunrise through coffee house windows.

Love has stolen my observance again,
replacing it with verse.

In a hundred ways
I resisted
the black and white winter nights,

but their patient beauty
woke me early,

forcing me
to that permanent spot
where the sky glows molten gold,
just before breath is suspended
in atmospheric pressure.

I am a twig
thrown onto your blaze.

In a puff of smoke
nothing remains
but emptiness
more beautiful than continuation.

This empty ocean,
the omnipresence of my childhood,
floods my existence,
drowning me in abstraction.

Words are no distraction.
They are ocean ripples
laughing at me.

Bathed in a sea of journeys,
who can stand in this tidal wave
and remember anything?

Luckily,
I am hidden away in this rural village
where no one remembers my name,
and the cost of living
is a peanut.

Flood

Love didn't come
with torrents of rainfall,
claps of thunder,
or rivers swelling their banks,
overwhelming homes and croplands.

Love came
like a mist on my face,
a warm spring day in Iowa,
cool in the glow of morning light,
dripping in sweat from honest surrender,
closing my eyes, refreshed.

Caring for soil and sun,
planting seeds
with open lips yielding no compromise
but the hint of a perfect summer,
and children,
born in the heartland.

Old

I can't help noticing
the signs of my growth,

creaks and whistles,
rusted hinges and calcified plumbing,
my wife, asleep at the wheel.

Transcendent breath,
freshly polished like a fire engine on parade day,
bleaches wicked thoughts
from contaminated global smog.

Fools of youth,
peel the pride from your eyes.
Nature does not mimic the littleness of men.

Strength
surrenders matter for enlargement;
like Christ or Buddha,
washing the sins of free will,

I need to pause a moment and howl.
The hue and texture of my parents' daylight
blinds and stuns my senses.

Maturity's final concert
obliterates the toxic waste
of childish cheers for martyrdom, revenge, and mur-
derous death penalties
by drinking deep into the ocean of souls
and surrendering all.

I need to pause again
and exhale my shame,
knees crumbling involuntarily.

Kneeling and impossibly suspended
by unutterable tears,
the exactness of my aging breath
and the unprejudiced glory of supernaturalism
exposes my reflection.

I am the voice of my father and the heart of my
mother,
who willing surrendered
so I may breathe awake.

Puppee

My father's life
was my lesson in endurance.
He went to a graveyard in Regina,
but not before he railed against the gates,
determined to bear noble infirmity
with merit.

He died in the arms of my dream,
like a plump infant.

I cradled him from afar,
without ever discovering
the seed of his origin.

He did not feel love
as his son felt it.

He understood what it meant to be alone.

Choosing an unpopular role,
performing well,
he departed to a standing ovation,
never heard.

Faithful

Silent soul,
holding me within,
shine faithfully
in the midst of rumbling billows.

Caress my skin
and hurl an invitation
to the hungry huddled,
frozen in fabricated pride.

Thunder
may alarm us,
but showers
will return us to the sea.

Birth

Don't try to keep what you own
to yourself.

Nature
who made you
won't hold a contract
demanding ownership,
turning a profit
on every act of creation.

Bangkok

When I see
a woman
well groomed,
I do not lust
long to possess
or control.

I am overtaken
with curiosity.

Why?

Why do I vibrate
at your sight?

1.
Hamilton, Near 12th Avenue

As a teen
I played my Hofner
near the corner of Hamilton and 12th,
collecting coins
…Fees for education.

One Saturday,
weary,
I sought recuperation
on a wall of bricks
…The Hudson Bay Company.

My mind sank,
addicted,
into my heart,
unaware of outside.

The hum of my soul escaped,
leaving me free of bodily urges and weight.

Above the sky
I heard my own accent whistling.

Without eyes or ears,
mouth or tongue,
I inhaled libraries,
reciting volumes
in nanoseconds,
until brash bus horns
stole my transcendence.

Like a bubble rising from the ocean floor,
I opened.

You looked into me
and spoke,

"Come to my workplace.
Tell me what you know of music."

"Yes Lord," sprung from my lips with ease,
and I shed my chrysalis.

Gathering my Hofner
and the coins in my case,
I followed the eyes that woke me.

Peacefully,
wc sat in a titanic bank office
...Toronto Dominion Bank of Canada.

I disclosed,

"Music is honest prayer,
nothing more."

You spoke,

"Today
I rested my eyes.
Out of the darkness
came bright daylight—
music, bright as laser beams
flooded my ears
and my fear of dying vanished.

Breathless,
a voice
both male and female
echoed in my heart.

'A schoolboy sleeps
near the corner
of Hamilton and 12th.
Remit your bonus to him.'"

"Sir,"
I spoke little by little,
one syllable at a time,
"I cannot accept."

"Son," he said.
"Sit here.
See the value of this remittance
sufficient to pay your tuition."

Realizing the generosity granted to me,
I remembered the hum of my soul.

"Thank you sir, but I cannot accept."

"Son, when someone's counting out currency for you,
don't look away."

"Sir, today
in a moment of rest,
I inhaled all that my young mind could comprehend;
I no longer seek importance.
Let's return to the corner of Hamilton and 12th.
Surely someone will be napping on bricks,
dreaming of you."

Eleven minutes,
we waited in silence
near the corner of Hamilton and 12th.

A young musician rose from his nap
and triggered a smile,
a vigor
magnetic
that lifted us
in selfless love.

There is no room for explanation
with love so strong.

It's the force
that draws a newborn
to mother's milk.

Near the corner of Hamilton and 12th,
"This day is done,"
I supposed to myself.
"I am no longer adolescent."

~

Four months passed;
October came.
Wet snow fell, breaking limbs.

Like a bird of instinct,
breathing Emerson and Thoreau,
I migrated
deep within the Catskill Range
…Livingston Manor, New York

2.
Livingston Manor, New York

I met you in Fallsburg—

a natural teacher
urging me to understand
the mystery
of self-identity,
replete with lineage, texts, tradition, and technique,
sharing life-waters with lovers and those willing.

In nature,
a newborn knows its family,
an ever-present bond
chronic like gravity.

You shone through me;
I felt warmth
like summer beach sand beneath my feet.

You barely spoke,
but I already knew what was happening.
I set off to Livingston Manor,
a drowning swimmer reaching shore.

Fourteen years
you emptied me,
teaching physics, math, physiology, and the rest.

To pay tuition,
pay respect,
I baked bread,
birthed calves,
repaired boilers,
gilded scripture,
raked sewers,
edited film,
pasteurized milk,
mastered ice cream,
printed to press.

You taught me
to gather skills
ahead of my competence,
by stretching time
and Being
absolutely present—

Mantras, Medicine, Ayurved, Jyotish,
Yoga, Architecture, Sama, Soma, Rik.

You taught me to write, lecture, teach,
and travel the world
with graduates.

You dressed me,
expanded me beyond comfort,
trained me to dine with popes and princes,
rich and mighty.

And by evening
serve the worthy,
swabbing dishes and scouring loos,
enriching the needy,
mending wounds,
instructing children.

In due course,
false pride fell aside
as fear always does
eventually.

Again,
full circle,
the hum of my soul
sails above the sky.

Again,
looking out
on a wistful world,
being in,
but not of,
a dream
which began
on the corner of Hamilton
near 12th Avenue,
nineteen seventy-four (~1974).

Courage and Dennis Gill

I first learned fear from my father—
an unnatural lesson
taught because I stole money
and couldn't tell time.

A grain of sand in a clamshell,
nurtured by time,
offers opportunity for priceless pearls,
harvested and cherished
one noble day:
    Imperial School
    Seventh grade
    Nineteen sixty-eight

    ~

Dennis,
leader of The Hard Rocks
(five fallen angels),
outnumbered Allan Lazerancco
with intimidation, size, and pretentious raw muscle.

Forecasting a predictable outcome,
more ashamed than afraid,
I coughed out a weak cliché,
clearly audible,
rich with distain,
"Why don't you pick on someone your own size?"

Yes,
it was rhetorical,
but The Hard Rocks
(a cranial emblem)
answered with a boot to my temple
and an equally cliché,
"Like you, jackass?"

The throbbing was mitigated
by Allan's honest respect
and my own.

The battle ended
with only a mild concussion
and the shrill ringing of the recess bell.

At 3:30
I gathered my books for home,
heading for the North door,
humming a mindless tune,
abruptly abridged
by a crowd of curious spectators
outside
eagerly awaiting
my blood.

Dennis smiled at me,
with nearly perfect teeth.

No explanation necessary.

I led the flock
to a nearby churchyard,
the customary battlefield
for abuse.

I keep secrets inside myself,
but today,
surrounded by a sea of Christians,
anticipating gladiators, blood, and diversion,
I stood sky clad—
full-frontal naked.

A fist to the side of my head was accompanied with,
"Fight, jackass!"

I remembered fear,
the fear of my father,
and time paused.

Then,
a surge.

I inhaled the rush to my bones,
awake to every blade of grass
and puff of breeze,
adrenaline waking a sleeping hulk.

This is the glory of war.
It enlightens every bodily receptor—
fully alive,
fully human,
urging us to crave greater risk
when its chemistry possesses us.

Acute,
Indomitable,
capable of annihilation, I need only will it.
Nothing could be easier

"I don't want to fight!"
I force past humiliation.

"Fight me, Chickenshit!"

Two added blows to my face
strengthen my resolve,
as blood from my nose flows down my canary yellow
shirtsleeves.

My gaze soaks my adversary,
now too fearful to look on.

"Why?"
I spit through the blood.

Unable to answer,
Dennis kicks me repeatedly
with his stylish, black pointed Rumble Boots
yelling, "Fight, asshole!"

Diffusing his slothful blows,
I uttered a syllable,
aiming to detonate
the blaze beneath his skin.

"No."

I relaxed my arms,
knowing the outcome.

His fists rupture both my nostrils.

Rich ruby blood
soaks every fiber of canary yellow,
frightening the Christians.

I knew then, this battle was done,
and my mind was already racing for the lie I resolved
to tell my mother.

"I was struck in the face playing football,"
was my settled invention.

It was three blocks
from the churchyard to my home.
Two concerned friends ambled with me,
nearly unable to speak.

I held my nostrils closed,
head cocked back.

They wanted to know.

Why?

Why I let Dennis hit me?

It took me every inch of three blocks
to answer;
"I don't want to be afraid anymore,"
I said,
keeping the secret to myself.
…victory

~

When you see through the eyes of someone you no
longer fear,
perspective revolves one hundred eighty degrees,
from black and white to Technicolor.

Fear is a curtain,
a veil we wear like sunglasses,
tinting perception
to bury humiliation.

~

When morning came, I was eager to show up for school,
no longer afraid of shame, my father, or Dennis.

School passed quickly.

At 3:30,
outside the North door,
the coliseum-crowd was waiting.

I led the way to the churchyard;

Dennis spoke with a fury of fists.

My answer was still "No."

Newly bruised and bloodied,
I knew a greater invention would be required to fool
my mother,
but maternal instinct
discerned the merit of falsehood
and she let me lie.

~

Thursday
mimicked Wednesday,
but the crowd was larger,
much larger,
and far more engaged.

North door
"Fight!"
"No!"
Blood
Abuse
Explanation to mum.

I knew my mother understood the lie,
understood the weight of war,
and she guarded my secret.

~

Friday was victory day.

The crowd was anxious,
restless,
but not for my blood.

Dennis sunk his right fist
into my left cheek,
frothing, "Fight me you scared jackass!"

His black onyx ring,
embellished with a gold letter G for Gill,
embedded itself deep beneath muscle tissue
near my left eye.

Too much inside, outside—
too much blood,
violence,
abuse.

An eruption of fright,
a collective gasp polluted the air.

Dennis struggled to unhinge his ring
from unyielding sinews holding tight.

One lucid tone,
a girl's voice,
uncontaminated and deeply penetrating,
echoed like an alpine horn at sunrise.

"Leave him alone!"

That was my initiation,
the first time I heard the music
of fearless abandonment.

It was Tamara's voice,
pregnant with conviction.

Without reference to any strand of wisdom,
I inhaled love from four directions.

Four dozen voices,
liberated,
standing like a wall of cannons,
pounded Dennis and The Hard Rocks.

The evidence of guilt,
the breach beneath my eye,
a bloodied fist,
ruby flesh, wedged in Gill's criminal ring.

I saw cowardice in his eyes—
confusion,
humiliation.

Everyone saw it.

War ends when we resolve it fearlessly.

I first learned this lesson from my father,
an unnatural lesson
taught because I stole money
and couldn't tell time.

But forgiveness
wrapped in a disguise of courage
taught me the currency of love,
the artistry of past and present starlight,
and how poetry leaves us no place to hide.

Overlooked

My dearest consort tells me
she is misunderstood,
unappreciated by kith and kin—
all the world.

Your voice is pretty,
like a morning bird,
but the patient stars hear each litigant,
bearing witness to all sides.

Mute with wisdom,
stars
say nothing,
and every plaintiff,
washed in the awe of starlight,
confesses nothing whatsoever
of injustice.

Circumambulate

Kodak moments,
Pacific to Atlantic,
seacoast to dessert.

Looking up,
where are my constellations?
Whose culture am I?

Show me your treasure,
faith and creed,
fear and love—
no knot of intellect,
but the eye in your heart.

Teach me
the forenames of your Goddess,
the first name of your Spirit,
the humming of your Soul.

Offer me
graciously
the hospitality of your tears,
the food that everyone wants.

Fasten all people together
and feel the pulse
that will not last
one hundred Springs.

We've come again
to the river
that pours through every soul,
stretching to the seacoast, unreachable by vessel—
bar thunder and silence.

I see a map
drawn in the lines of every palm,
leading in unlikely directions
to inexhaustible treasure
implicitly familiar
to every part of us.

MERS 2014

MERS
reminds me
we are all bound.

Reminds me,
individuals do not evolve;
populations evolve.

Asleep at night,
I ponder the prayers of three billion Christians,
two billion Muslims,
one billion Hindus,
one hundred and sixty million atheists,
and the rest.

A symphony of perfection
ranked equal
by God,
deaf to human language,
keen for humility.

Does God profit from confession
or augment from praise?

Do you?

Spiritual impotence,
a mortal epidemic,
is remiss
of honest praise,
remiss
of breath suspended.

MERS
reminds me
we are related.

Reminds me
individuals do not evolve;
populations evolve.

The CIA's World Factbook gives world population as 7,021,836,029 (July 2012 est.) and the distribution of religions as Christian 33.39% (of which Roman Catholic 16.85%, Protestant 6.15%, Orthodox 3.96%, Anglican 1.26%), Muslim 22.74%, Hindu 13.8%, Buddhist 6.77%, Sikh 0.35%, Jewish 0.22%, Baha'i 0.11%, other religions 10.95%, non-religious 9.66%, atheists 2.01%

Zen Master

I met you
long ago,
a laborer
working at a distance
like me.

Something in your movements
caught my eye—
confident,
unstrained,
natural,
like a Midwest doe.

Compelled to know,
I came to your work site
to talk.

Shiny with honest perspiration,
you greeted me like an honored guest.
I couldn't mistake your vitality
or the stillness of your demeanor.

We introduced ourselves,
seated on freshly cut grass,
with stories and laughter,
every moment
charged with supernaturalism
and the buzzing of overfed honey bees.

Three hours passed,
like a moment in love.

Your courage astonished me,
my mouth fell starstruck
when I realized
your National Geographic celebrity.

Thankful for each other,
we parted ways.

You returned to your work,
I to mine.

I read about you later
in books and magazines;

I visited the monuments
of your accomplishments.

I still see you on the streets.

Occasionally
we pass each other on bikes;
you always nod back at me
but I don't think you remember my name.

You suppose
I'm a celebrity or a scholar,
but I'm a laborer,
a biker
like you.

When we pass,
I am warm and calm
with moistened eyes.

You radiate a tangible hygiene.

With seven swollen tears,
I wonder,
does anyone know
the fame of your guileless humility?
And the journey
you endured alone,
to become an honest heart
mastering every ocean?

Either way,
beauty surrounds us,
and sometimes, bathed in admiration,
we are shown
what's hidden
in a treasured poem.

Snob

I cannot sit
through another sermon;
explanations and awkward metaphors
are a source of indigestion and heartburn.

Let the waves crash over me.

I'll grow gills
and build a home in this salty sea.

The gospel of imitation
just lulls me to sleep.

Tall Steps Forward

"I haven't grown much today;"
I often fool myself into believing
something's new.

But I can't give you wings,
I only know a few words.

Ask the tea master;
she knows what it means
to die for love.

Through the Looking Glass

I'm staring at myself
in the mirror again,
and everyone inside
is staring back.

Some of you
will understand my meaning;
some
will think I'm mad.

Mirrors
are brilliant metaphors,
reflecting back
everything we offer.

Those
full of conviction
fall in love with themselves—
unaltercd,
fetching honor for their ancestors.

Fatherhood

One memory
I cannot resolve,
is the irrepressible esteem
stainless in your eyes
as you witness me pass.

Only Jesus
has shown me
equal masculine valor.

Surpassing
the right hand of God
with overwhelming humility,
the radiance of your adoration
rips open the sky at will,
clearing obstacles,
granting infinities
impossible to comprehend.

And all that ever was, is, or could be
exists
in a particle of love,
the reflection
in your eyes
that I choose
to never resolve.

Helix

I woke
with moonlight shining
in my eyes—
a total eclipse,
nearly complete.

I remembered
a world in bondage—
invisible prison walls
constructed with
violence, denial, poverty, addiction, and lies.

But spring
is wearing its intoxicating fragrance,
causing me to frolic
rich with hope
for open-minded continuations,
free of superstition,
sloth, and half-thoughts.

No planet
can eclipse
your soul.

It's just a shadow.

Fairfield Again

We've lived in this cornfield
for a quarter century,
watching each other
live and die.

I know it bothers you
when I say so,
but it's precious to me—
all the seasons of the year,
the clothes we wear,
and the wonder of fruition.

Wall Street Dealer

No one is fooled for long
by insider information.
These are the secrets
children tell each other.

With familiarity,
dealers
buff up their wallets.

Current trends
find billionaires,
bullish to burnished merit.

Thank god,
there is more to want
than fame, riches,
and graveyard dust.

If Earth
were your true mother,
what gift would you offer?

She already owns
the minerals that make you.

Hall of Dignity

Jesus,
you're in my dreams again.

Washing my feet—
a wonder of creation.

You allege
my feet reek.

I say,
"Look who's talking?
You're two thousand years old
and wearing the same clothes."

Snorting
like a baby calf,
you tackle me,
forcing my face into freshly cut grass.

Seven times, battering me
before I flip You off,
struggling to locate your weakness.

Laughing and swearing
like brothers,
tumbling forward,
exhausted,
I surrender.

You are strong,
but I live to fight tomorrow.

Struggling with You
teaches me mercy,
and the folly of casting stones.

Gabbing about lucidity,
You allege
my dreams are dull, robotic, and colorless—
like my poems.

Pissed,
I condescend,
"You're volatile,
lack management skills,
and WHAT have You ever written worth reading?"

Encouraging me with laughter,
I thank God You appreciate
the defects
that hide in dreams.

Obedient Cleric

Adhering to obedience,
did you miss simplicity?

Your eyes are open wide,
like an eager child.

You write poems
that breath beauty,
tickling invisible laughter.

Ungrateful,
your obedience
turns love to rust,
youth to dust.

Like a child,
obey simple love.
Simple is best.

Friends

Today,
pause
and let the winter sun
cozy your face.

Most of our Springs
are behind us now.

In retrospect,
surviving our failings
is a permanent victory.

Don't waste time
pondering the value
of so short a life.

There are oceans to cross,
and strong intentions
for our children's potential.

Rebirth

Time to unload.
Empty your bags;
don't be afraid of the chill.

All that weight,
too familiar,
just lies we tell ourselves.

Let go.
Promise yourself generosity.

It's easier
than what's imagined.

Claiming Artistry

I'll invent new words
to honor
living.

Without commands,
hearts beat,
lungs fill with air,
eyes squint
to rhythms
that reach beyond our skin and bones.

An instant
subsumed,
in step with inspiration,
directing planet and atom,
cannot be understood
through human genius.

But we can hum and whistle
and listen in awe,
inventing nothing at all
with honor.

Autonomic

Fortunately,
my body
takes care of itself.

I have never
scheduled a heartbeat,
breath, or blink.

Hair, skin, and nails
preserve integrity
without my vote.

Hungry, my tummy grumbles.
Thirsty, a space below my tongue
signals an unmistakable urge.

Recharging my battery, I'm asleep on the sofa
to sitcoms, news, and children's laughter.

Still,
I am free
to disobey
the autonomy
that organizes me.

DO

Today I turned around
and saw an old friend.

His words are easy to understand;
there are no lies here.

He claims ownership
of only one thing—
the love he bears is free will.

I have no control over love.
It does what it wants with me,
asking only
that I polish its facets.

Holding Your Breath

Fearful of being robbed?

Don't postpone it.
Invite the thief
to steal away
with your most cherished secrets.

Living has no greater gift.

Mako

Again,
I cannot stop this howling.

A husky
alone in the heat of noon
craves his master's cooling touch.

The sweetness of this moaning
points me to that territory
so familiar,
it's impossible to understand how I ever became lost.

This wild abandonment
is a noisy devotion,
but mercy,
like nature,
rushes to consume the helpless,
all the while
illuminating the origin of manly vigor.

I cannot stop this howling;
it's proof of mercy.

Desires

When the sky opens,
you will be granted all mercies.

Ask for anything.

Non-toxic,
your success is assured.

The trick is knowing what to ask for.

Unaware,
poor men pray for money,
blind men for sight.

Weary for sleep,
the restless ask for sex and war.

Those well-rested,
already home,
rally the willing,
knowing inspiration is natural,
like a warm breeze on a bare body.

On Earth,
as in heaven.

Fitness

Don't waste time on normalcy.
Death oscillates like an Iowa winter;
take the balance
and nourish the spirit you imagine.

Capture the King

Today
I am a pawn
in this Chess game.

But yesterday,
I moved diagonally,
a bishop
devouring the castle of linearity.

A quarter century ago,
I was a black king,
who took a white queen
in check.

I learned
the only valid counter
is checkmate,
and that chess is not a game,
but an art, each piece
knowing its performance,
subject
to clarity and presence.

Every Day a Miracle Happens

I tried to write,
believing
without a doubt
I could.

I prayed industriously,
devoting hundreds of dark dawns,
renovating the world with every written word,
borrowing generously,
avoiding disguise.

I reviewed my mischief daily
at 3:00 AM,
devouring fresh oven biscuits
at Hardee's on highway 34.

Like a baby, I wrote—
still do.

My role models, unorthodox scholars,
thought I was giving,
but I was receiving, each page
a miracle,
a familiar confirmation.

For fifteen minutes
I knew fame,
with a faceless crowd
chanting my name,
lusting importance
and world energies.

But charity
found its way,
granting humility.

Stain glass idols
became human beings—
joyful
in abrupt insolvency.

And knowing
Nature is everywhere,
the poet
became Nature.

Divergence

My turtlemate
tells me
I twist everything
inside out.

She's right.

I see the world
different than I once did.

An hour before dawn
my soul is drawn
into the sun,
where my notions
are turned to ash.

All that I ever knew,
just fertilizer for new growth

Some say
I'm brainwashed
or self-deluded.

But fear,
the root of criticism,
is dissonant,

and self-honesty
has a different sound—
clean
and easily heard.

I do not stand among those
who memorize
the standard of conformity.

I do not see them before the dawn.

Absorbed in denial,
shackled with iron beliefs,
practicing love
in small, safe circles,

an hour before dawn,
willing or unwilling,
the sun
subsumes you,

and all notions
but pervading love
are turned to ash.

Balance

How do I measure myself?
With what scale?

The omniscience
that shaped my bones
from billion year old stardust,
gathered all my senses
with the strings that make them play,
to orchestrate this masterpiece.

By this measure,
I am not a note,
or a space between,
or a memory,
or a hint.

Hint of Divorce

It began
in my breath,
half a century past.

My in-law father,
a libertine,
young and debonair,
rich with infidelity,
overexerted his adultery,
tearing the fabric of sister and spouse.

Wealth, inheritance, and privilege,
gamble more liberally,
accommodating risks
unknown to common men.

Divorce, business-like,
is affordable,
and easily managed,
but betrayal,
never resting,
colors the world grey
with self-pity.

The seed of divorce
began here,
breeding genetic disposition,
and the lie
that mankind is false
and womankind weak.

I dreamt of this weakness
and dismissed it,
believing austerity would triumph.
But who can swim
against a frozen current for twenty-five years?

In due course,
hypothermia will kill you,
germinating new seeds
of cause and divorce.

Yield

The artist in me
is tethered by gold chains
to a small circle of desperate shipmates.

We are fated
to scrape beneath the facets of our armor.

The ones that hold us
abandoned,
rafting ocean waves,
waiting to be rescued,
unwilling to drown in beauty.

Turtlely

A chatterbox
repetitious as tooth decay.

She says,
"Many will howl when I go."

Like a comedian I ask,
"Where?"

Those who'll weep
live within this turtle shell,
which travels with me everywhere.

Lord,
I trust you to extinguish this candle
with the same magic that gave it light.

Stickman

Towering by daybreak,
assembling notes,
eating little,

loving a good deal,
knowing what is right,
eloquent,
bowing to everyone, loved and willing,

touching the ocean's belly,
outshining imagination,
light as gossamer,

clap and sing with pulse and meter;
Drum Son,

each beat
built with well-winds,
purpose, adventure, and rhyme.

Drum Son.

Free

What's it like, fear?

Owning everything,
needing nothing,
but this moment
and its precious sunrise.

Don't let prayer
be your prison.

Listen.

Dust

Not again.
More tears.

Today
I heard children's voices
reading your poems.

Some read beyond my limit;
some read below it;
some, have never taken notice of inner music.

Either way,
we are dancing,
like dust grains in sunbeams.

Legend

So in love,
I have hidden your name in everything.

When I tell you I am drunk,
you know my intoxication is you.

When I tell you I am empty,
you know my vacancy has no beginning or end.

In the rain,
I am soaked in ravishment.

Grumbling,
you are absent.

Hunger and thirst (newly born),
I panic without the prospect of you.

Alone,
I have abandoned you.

Selfish lovers
recite prayers and holy names,
hopeful for boons.

But impotent,
they remain barren,
like scriptures
in the hands of infants.

"And it must follow, as the night the day,
Thou canst not then be false to any man."

Parenting werewolves,
akin to salmon raging upriver for the spawn,
ends in death and new birth.

Angry,
I ask you,
"How long
to unravel the flawed,
soulless education
enforced by law?"

Teen wolves,
run free,
inhale the virility of your forefathers,

define the freshness
in the middle of your chest.

Listen to the music master
who merits you
by the vitality of your tone.

And be true
to the image you imagine.

Bitter Sweet

May I nuzzle you
with self-expression
and jazz guitar
lost in meter,
timeless.

Why lovers
waste time
throwing stones at mirrors
is clear.

They're unfamiliar
that reflection shatters
with the force of self-identity.

Collect

Eyes to see
Ears to hear
Skin fondles everything
My salty tongue wags nonstop
What does my soul collect?

Overshadowed

Personating a mother,
ancient or vogue,
I seek to offer
what I did not grasp.

Personating a father,
I am weak
when you ask,
will I bless this marriage.

Words
stop working.

I ask,

"Will you die content,
drunk with molten gold?
Will he drink tea with you,
hold your hand,
make you laugh?"

I'll wait with you
until the moment
I hold you again,
no longer needing to exhale.

Front Page News

In my family
we are four,
with hundreds of destinations
not always compatible.

Nonetheless,
together,
helpful,
our many goals are realized
with ease.

Signs

Fledgling fathers
hoist their darlings overhead,
buoyant that their greenhorn will outshine Osiris.

As it should be.

This mystery of life
unravels itself
with signs and symbols directly in front of you,
from dusk to dawn,
where you'll wake up laughing
that death ever worried you at all.

Resistance

No one saddles a bull with abuse.

It takes skill—matured
tried and true technique,
evolved, like jazz,
improvisational.

Sweet yams,
gentle words
and patience,
initiate this journey
safely.

Nature chooses the path of least resistance
for good reason.

Trust yourself when I tell you,
heroes honor those
who rid themselves of false pride.

About the Author

I've overheard a contemporary voice,
the murmur of poets,
impatient to elevate the balance of sharing,
offering sacred time,
shoving boulders uphill,
over the top,
gathering momentum with every downhill sway.

Unforced verse,
and unrestricted crosswinds
hoist a sail of hope.

Your hope.

Like storybook marines, being all,
defending the crumbling constitution of trust.

Also available

The Meter is Irregular
Volume 1
Parenting Teenage Werewolves

The Meter is Irregular
Volume 2
Unleashing Teenage Werewolves

www.ingramcontent.com/pod-product-compliance
Lightning Source LLC
Chambersburg PA
CBHW022036090426
42741CB00007B/1093